Extraordinary Extinct™
Crystal Palace Dinosaurs

Jill Michelle Smith

and

Jennifer Watson

Rock face

Hylaeosaurus head ✗

Palaeozoic rocks

② Labyrinthodon
③ Icthyosaurus
④ Plesiosaurus
⑥ Megalosaurus
⑧ Iguanodon
⑦ Hylaeosaurus
① Dicynodon
⑤ Teleosaurus
⑨ Pterodactyl
⑩ Mosasaurus

Landscaped by Joseph Paxton and David Thomas Ansted in 1854

⑫ Anoplotherium

Victorian Boating Lake

Permian	Triassic	Jurassic	Cretaceous
299 MYA	252 million years ago	201 million years ago	145 million years ago

The Geological Court at Crystal Palace Park

Opened by Queen Victoria and Prince Albert in 1854,
At a time before anyone had even heard of a dinosaur.
The Geological Court gave the whole world a new insight,
As the study of palaeontology revealed ancient life.
With extraordinary extinct creatures for visitors to find,
The landscape of the park was a journey though time!

This way to where the Crystal Palace once stood

⑪ Palaeotherium

Tertiary Island

⑬ Megatherium

⑭ Megaloceros

Palaeogene	Neogene	Quarternary
6 million years ago	23 million years ago	2.58 million years ago (to modern day)

Georges Cuvier

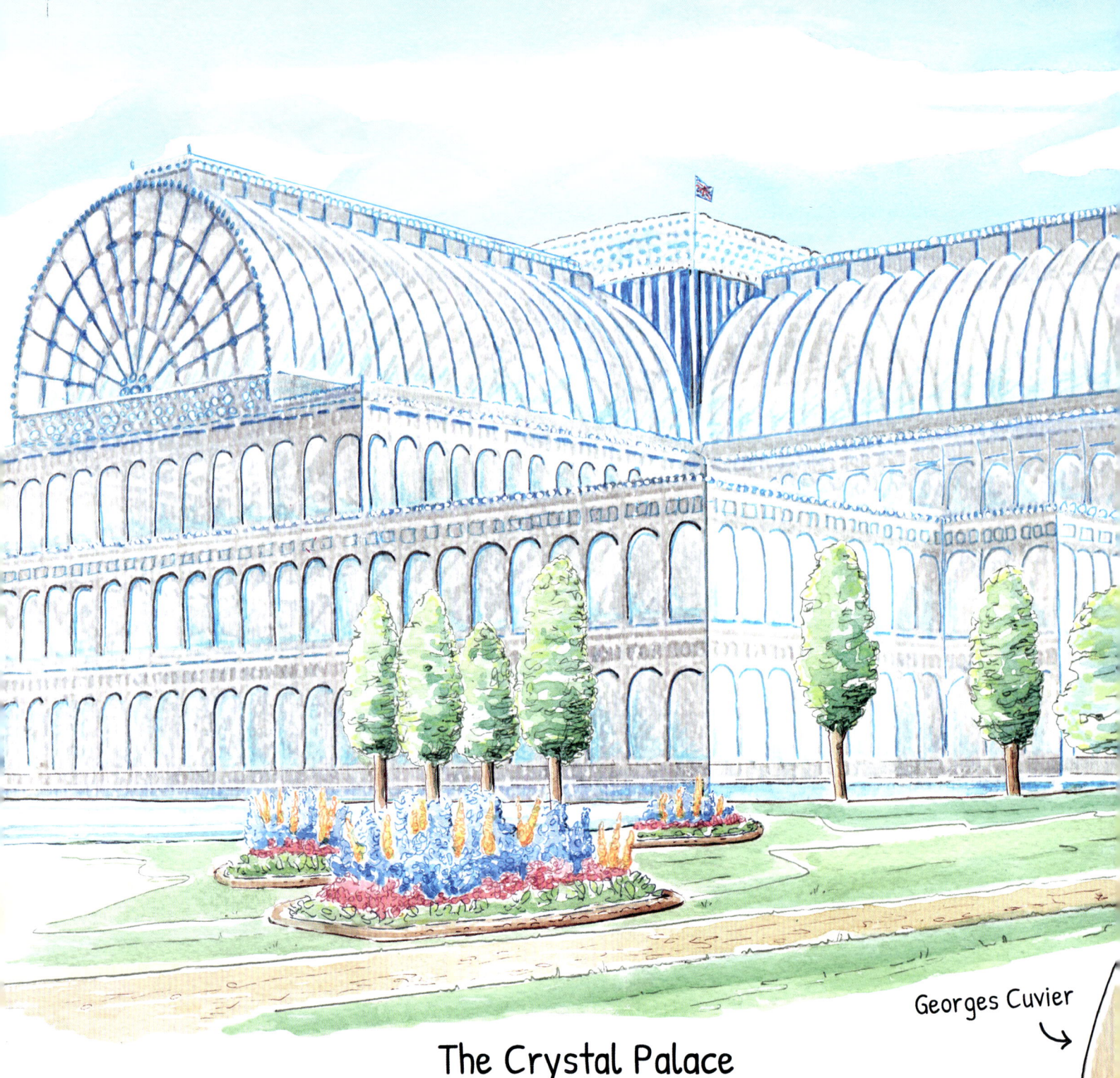

The Crystal Palace

The Great Exhibition in Hyde Park was the grandest there had been,
Displaying great wonders of the world most people had never seen!
After the lavish fair had ended, it was moved from London's heart,
And the gleaming glasshouse was built again in Crystal Palace Park.
Amongst the greenery of the grounds a prehistoric land took shape,
With two hundred million years of history constructed around the lake.

Pioneering People

The discovery of terrible lizards and sea serpents from long ago,
Combined with new science and thinking, would create quite the show.
Although Mantell was asked first, Owen advised on the planning,
With extra insights from Darwin, Buckland, Cuvier and Anning.
Guided by this, Waterhouse Hawkins took on the remarkable feat,
To sculpt a menagerie of extinct beasts, ready for all to meet!

Mary Ann Mantell

Gideon Mantell

Mary Anning

Richard Owen

William Buckland

Charles Darwin

Benjamin Waterhouse Hawkins

Dicy the Dicynodon

Pronounced: *die-sin-oh-don*

Extinct: 252 million years ago   Size: 3.6 metres long

First there was tusk-toothed Dicy, a creature hard to ignore,
As she greeted startled spectators from the Permian shore.
Although her strange shape was a bit of a mistake,
A link between reptiles and mammals she'd make.
Basking in the sunshine like a half turtle, half walrus,
It was curious to think of what once lived before us!

Lawrence the
Labyrinthodon

Pronounced: *la-buh-rinth-oh-don*

Extinct: 235 million years ago   Size: 2.6 metres long

Lawrence was so monstrous that the Victorians would quake,
As soon as they saw him paddling his toes in the lake.
His amphibian features and glassy froggy glare,
Were enough to make anyone stop and stare!
He had two Triassic sidekicks, one with much smoother skin,
But he was humpy and bumpy with the toothiest grin.

Pearl the Plesiosaurus

Pronounced: *plee-see-oh-saw-rus*

Extinct: 191 million years ago   Size: 4 metres long

Beached on the bank, a bit further into the Court,
Pearl was a marine reptile, a sea serpent of sorts.
Discovered by Mary Anning, when fossils were hard to believe,
As surely there wasn't life on Earth long before Adam and Eve?
In those days, women were rarely recognised for their finds,
But such impressive beasts as these couldn't be brushed aside!

Iris the Ichthyosaurus

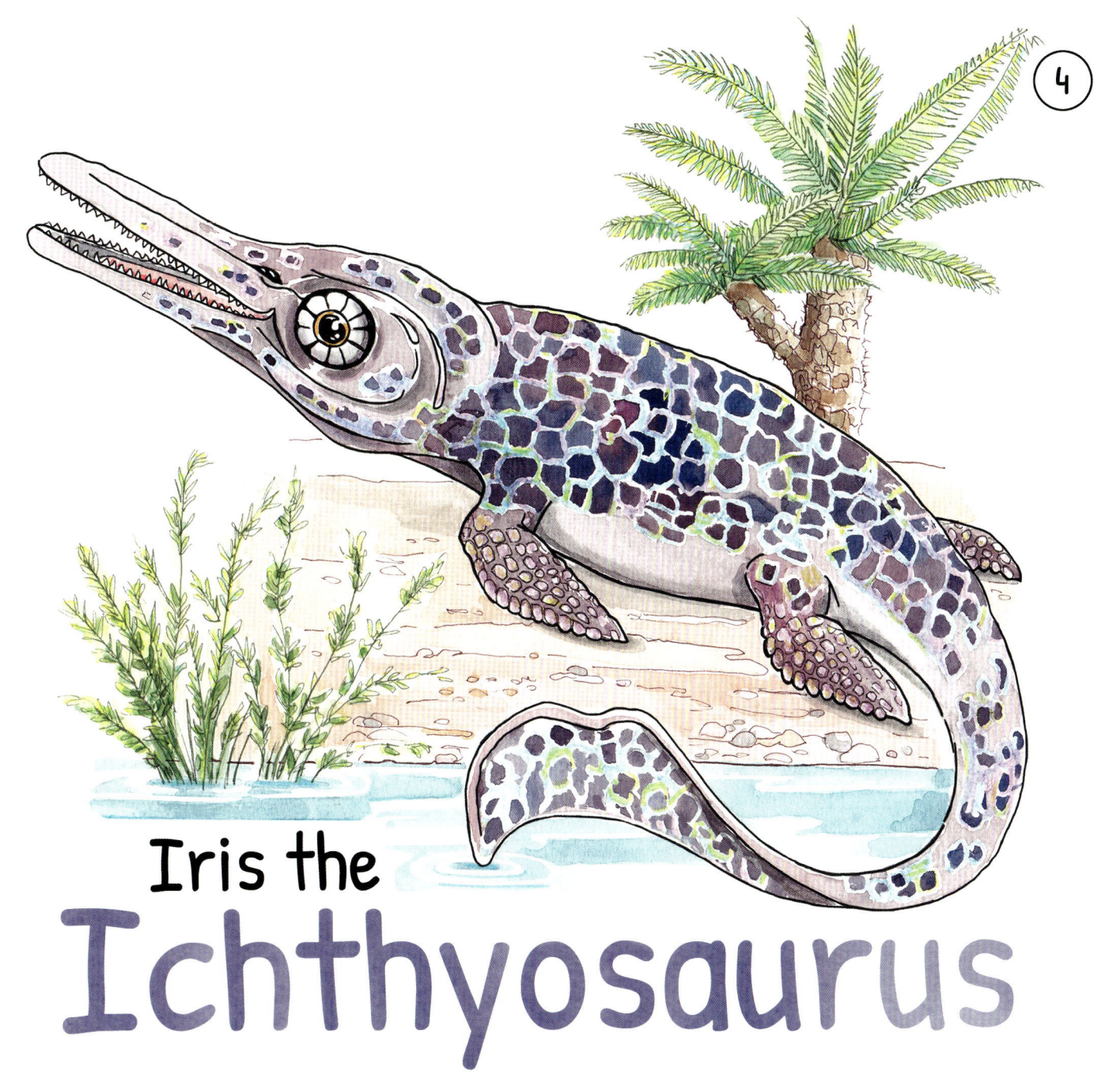

Pronounced: *ick-thee-oh-saw-rus*

Extinct: 185 million years agoSize: 12 metres long

With her swishy, fishy tail slinking in the pool beside,
Iris was a swimming reptile, with huge sclerotic eyes.
Mary Anning had discovered an enormous skull many years before,
So it was stunning to show these Leviathan looks and bottle-nosed jaw.
In the ocean, a Jurassic sea dragon would have been to fear,
But while stranded like a whale on land, she couldn't have come near!

Terrence the
Teleosaurus

Pronounced: *tee-lee-oh-saw-rus*

Extinct: 164 million years ago   Size: 8 metres long

What must have been thought of this crocodilian creature?
With his nose in the air, Terrence was a fabulous feature.
His fossils were dug from the craggy cliffs of Yorkshire,
And now in the lake his reptilian shape did appear.
With his extra wide grin and his tail length even greater,
He looked a lot like a super-stretched alligator!

Meg the Megalosaurus

Pronounced: *meg-ah-low-saw-rus*

Extinct: 166 million years ago   Size: 10.7 metres long

The sight of Meg must have been a frightful thing for sure,
As no one had ever seen a dinosaur before!
She had a frosty fearsome frown and tooth-packed snarly jaws,
Her arching back posed attack as she stood firmly on all fours.
Before science and natural history, religion had been taught,
But now this monster was revealed, new answers would be sought.

Heidi the Hylaeosaurus

Pronounced: *hi-lee-oh-saw-rus*

Extinct: 133 million years ago   Size: 8.4 metres long

Her curling smile would always make Heidi quite the charmer,
Even though across her form she was clad with spikes and armour!
Piecing together her skeleton was such a tricky task,
That it was rather hard to be confident about her shape and stance.
So Waterhouse Hawkins made the decision to keep her facing away,
And her original stone head can now be found atop the hill today.

Iggy the Iguanodon

Pronounced: *ig-wah-noh-don*

Extinct: 110 million years ago   Size: 9.6 metres long

After Mary Ann Mantell recovered teeth from a rocky roadside,
A world of dinosaurs would be revealed when Iggy was identified.
About this ancient creature though, the scientists didn't agree;
Plodding along, sturdy and strong, or reclined against a tree?
So two prehistoric beasts were made to capture each position,
But placing a thumb spike on his nose remains an odd decision!

Petra the
Pterodactyl

Pronounced: *terr-oh-dak-til*

Extinct: 66 million years ago   Size: 5 metres wide

Resembling a swan with lizard toes and plenty of sharp teeth,
Petra was like a scaly gargoyle looming over the park beneath.
Perching on rocks, the idea of lift off would have seemed outrageous,
But pterosaurs really did rule the skies during the late Cretaceous.
Her curvy companion sat by her side with peculiar folded wings,
The Victorians must have surely admired such fantastical flying things!

Moses the Mosasaurus

Pronounced: *mow-sah-saw-rus*

Extinct: 66 million years ago   Size: 9 metres long

This seemingly mythical monster was unearthed by the River Meuse,
When Moses was made, it was conveyed that such sea creatures were true.
He had two rows of teeth in his vast upper jaws like a gigantic snake,
Though his twisting tail can only be imagined thrashing in the lake.
A biblical beast, a worrisome wonder to find in the depths of the park,
A splendid surprise for his audience to spy, especially after dark!

Pierre the Palaeotherium

Pronounced: *pay-lee-oh-theer-ee-um*

Extinct: 34 million years ago   Size: 2 metres long

Pierre was found in Paris when his fossils were exhumed,
Where the city was to stand, a great forest once grew.
He had three toes like a rhino and a trunk a bit like an elephant's,
With rugged, stripy skin to suit the warm Eocene elements.
A strange mix between a tapir and short, sturdy pony,
Alongside his smaller relatives, he was never lonely!

Angelina the Anoplotherium

Pronounced: *an-op-loh-theer-ee-um*

Extinct: 34 million years ago   Size: 3.6 metres long

Another discovery in Paris was soon to be found,
When fossils of Angelina were dug from the ground.
She had a head like a camel and was created to stand,
Looking over the water from the Tertiary Island.
She was strongly built, like a donkey or sheep,
With an extra long tail and four hooved feet.

Mateo the Megatherium

Pronounced: *meg-ah-theer-ee-um*

Extinct: 9,000 years ago   Size: 5 metres tall

Mateo once roamed sandy plains where his fossils were found within,
And sent across the sea to England by the famous Charles Darwin.
A huge and hairy ground sloth towering high into the trees,
Stretching for a leafy lunch, which he could have seized with ease.
Much bigger than his cousins that are still around today,
This mighty mammal made a most magnificent display!

Magnus the Megaloceros

Pronounced: *meg-ah-low-seh-ross*

Extinct: 8,000 years ago   Size: 3.5 metres long

Guided by bones collected in Ireland from the last Ice Age,
Magnus and his giant deer family were met with accolade!
His proportions were perfect and with real antlers he was adorned,
With so much known about him, the Victorians were well informed.
He looked towards his visitors with a noble, stately stare,
His species lived all around the world as we are now aware.

On this exciting expedition for visitors to discover,
Most of the sculptures were grouped alongside others.
Specially positioned to show habitat and motion,
With much clever guesswork based on scientific notions.
Masterfully crafted from concrete, brick and wire,
Across three centuries they have continued to inspire!

The two Iguanodon sculptures

The original Hyaelosaurus head

The mysterious Xiphodon (zy-foe-don) sculpture among the giant deer

Crystal Palace Park is a triumph of natural history,
Although much about the creatures still remains a mystery.
Like the puzzle of the species seen lying on the lawn,
Which for many years was thought to be the giant deer's fawn.
This gangly, long necked mammal has now been confirmed,
Proving how much more there is still to be learned!

Discover what scientists today think the Crystal Palace creatures might have looked like!

Before the Dinosaurs

Dicynodon ①
"Two Canine Teeth"

Lived: Permian
Size: 1.5 metres long
Diet: plants and vegetation
First discovered: South Africa
Named by: Richard Owen, 1845

Therapsids, like *Dicynodon*, were ancestors of mammals and evolved before the first dinosaurs appeared in the Triassic Period.

Labyrinthodon ②
"Maze Tooth"

Lived: Triassic
Size: 6 metres long
Diet: fish and smaller amphibians
First discovered: Warwickshire, England
Named by: Richard Owen, 1842

Although Richard Owen tried to rename this ancient amphibian, it is actually known as Mastodonsaurus! (mass-tuh-don-saw-rus)

Marine Reptiles

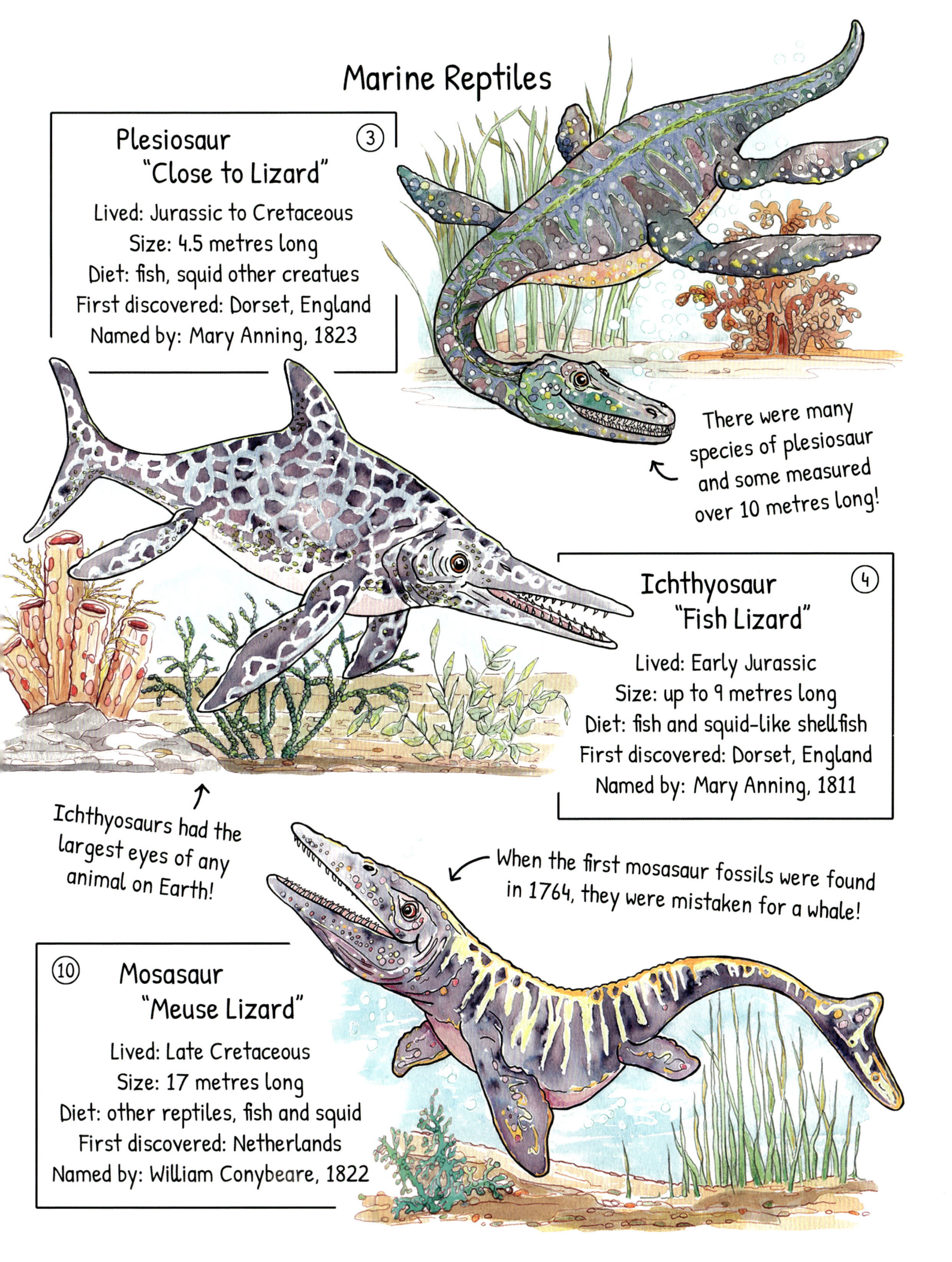

Plesiosaur ③
"Close to Lizard"

Lived: Jurassic to Cretaceous
Size: 4.5 metres long
Diet: fish, squid other creatues
First discovered: Dorset, England
Named by: Mary Anning, 1823

There were many species of plesiosaur and some measured over 10 metres long!

Ichthyosaur ④
"Fish Lizard"

Lived: Early Jurassic
Size: up to 9 metres long
Diet: fish and squid-like shellfish
First discovered: Dorset, England
Named by: Mary Anning, 1811

Ichthyosaurs had the largest eyes of any animal on Earth!

When the first mosasaur fossils were found in 1764, they were mistaken for a whale!

⑩ Mosasaur
"Meuse Lizard"

Lived: Late Cretaceous
Size: 17 metres long
Diet: other reptiles, fish and squid
First discovered: Netherlands
Named by: William Conybeare, 1822

Dinosaurs

⑥ Megalosaurus
"Giant Lizard"

Lived: Middle Jurassic
Size: 9 metres long
Diet: other dinosaurs, such as sauropods
First discovered: Oxfordshire, England
Named by: William Buckland, 1824

✶ Richard Owen introduced the word 'Dinosaur' in 1842, it means "Terrible Lizard".

Hylaeosaurus ⑦
"Forest Lizard"

Lived: Early Cretaceous
Size: 7.5 metres long
Diet: a variety of plants
First discovered: Sussex, England
Named by: Gideon Mantell, 1833

⑧ Iguanodon
"Iguana Tooth"

Lived: Early Cretaceous
Size: 10 metres long
Diet: vegetation and fruits
First discovered: Sussex, England
Named by: Gideon Mantell, 1825

Found by Mary Ann Mantell in 1822, *Iguanodon* was the first dinosaur to be discovered, but second to be named.

Pterosaurs and Crocodilians

Pterodactyl ⑨
"Winged Finger"

Lived: Triassic to Cretaceous
Size: 6 metre average wingspan
Diet: fish and smaller reptiles
First discovered: Bavaria, Germany
Named by: Georges Cuvier, 1809

Pterodactylus antiquus was the first pterosaur discovered in 1784. It had a 1 metre wing span.

Teleosaurus ⑤
"Perfect Lizard"

Lived: Middle Jurassic
Size: 3 metres long
Diet: fish, squid and small animals
First discovered: Yorkshire, England
Named by: William Buckland, 1824

Although Georges Cuvier gave the name 'pterodactyl' to flying reptiles in general, scientists today now use 'pterosaur' to better describe this very large and varied group!

Believe it or not, these ancient reptiles are not directly related to modern crocodiles!

Early Modern Mammals

Palaeotherium ⑪
"Ancient Beast"

Lived: Eocene Epoch (Palaeogene Period)
Size: 2 metres long
Diet: soft fruit and leaves
First discovered: Paris, France
Named by: Georges Cuvier, 1804

There are three species in Crystal Palace Park; *Palaeotherium magnum, medium* and *minus* (big, medium and small!)

* *Palaeotherium* and *Anoplotherium* were two of the first extinct creatures in history to be recognised from fossils.

Although the Crystal Palace anoplotheres are on all fours, it is now believed that they could reach high branches by stretching up on two legs and using their strong tail to balance - a bit like a kangaroo!

Anoplotherium ⑫
"Unarmed Beast"

Lived: Eocene Epoch (Palaeogene Period)
Size: up to 3 metres tall
Diet: a variety of plants, leaves and fruit
First discovered: Paris, France
Named by: Georges Cuvier, 1804

Prehistoric Megafauna

Megatherium ⑬
"Giant Beast"

Lived: Pliocene to Pleistocene Epoch
(Neogne to Quaternary Period)
Size: 6 metres tall
Diet: fibrous plants and fruit
First discovered: Argentina
Named by: Georges Cuvier, 1796

During the voyage of the HMS Beagle, Charles Darwin collected giant sloth fossils from South America, in 1832. These helped inspire his theory of evolution, as well as Benjamin Waterhouse Hawkins' sculpture.

Megaloceros ⑭
"Great Horn"

Lived: Pleistocene to Holocene Epoch
(Quaternary Period)
Size: 3 metres long with antlers 3.5 metres wide
Diet: grass, foliage and tree leaves
First discovered: Ireland
Named by: Johann Friedrich Blumenbach, 1799

Over the last 400 years many fossils and even some cave paintings have been found of these enormous deer!

Dodo and Dinosaur®

Discover the Extraordinary Extinct™ emporium...

dodoanddinosaur.com

Extraordinary Extinct™
Crystal Palace Dinosaurs

By purchasing this book, you are helping to conserve the Crystal Palace Dinosaurs for future generations.

First published in the UK in 2023

Text copyright © 2023 Jill Michelle Smith and Jennifer Watson
Illustrations copyright © 2023 Jill Michelle Smith
Copyright © 2023 Dodo and Dinosaur®

Written by Jill Michelle Smith and Jennifer Watson
Illustrated by Jill Michelle Smith
Designed by Jennifer Watson

With special thanks to Sarah Jayne, Ellinor Michel, Mark Witton and the Friends of Crystal Palace Dinosaurs.
The Friends of Crystal Palace Dinosaurs is a registered charity, no.1165231

Printed on 100% sustainably sourced, Carbon Balanced paper by Barnwell Print Ltd in association with World Land Trust.
Helping to preserve critically threatened tropical rainforests.

WORLD LAND TRUST™
www.carbonbalancedprinter.com
Barnwell Print Reg. No. 2102
CBP019743

A catalogue record of this book is available from the British Library.

No part of this publication may be reproduced, stored in a retrieval system, or transmitted in any form, or by any means, electrical, mechanical, photocopying, recording or otherwise, without the prior written permission of the authors.

All rights reserved. Dodo and Dinosaur® is a registered trademark.
Extraordinary Extinct™ is a trademark of Dodo and Dinosaur® and is protected by common law.